First published in 2007
by Wayland

Copyright © Wayland 2007

Wayland
338 Euston Road
London NW1 3BH

Wayland Australia
Hachette Children's Books
Level 17/207 Kent Street
Sydney, NSW 2000

British Library Cataloguing in Publication Data
Walker, Kathryn, 1957-
   Cat. - (See how they grow)
   1. Cats - Juvenile literature
   2. Kittens - Juvenile literature
   I. Title
   636.8'07

ISBN-13: 978 0 7502 5252 2

Printed in China
Wayland is a division of Hachette Children's Books.

The publishers would like to thank the following
for allowing us to reproduce their pictures in
this book:
Corbis: 14 (Cecilia Enholm/Etsa), 17
(K & H Benser/zefa), 21 (Jim Craigmyle). FLPA:
cover (Konrad Wothe/ Minden Pictures), 5
(Flip de Nooyer/Foto Natura), 6 (Tony Hamblin),
9 (Angela Hampton), 15 (Mitsuaki Iwago/Minden
Pictures), 19 (Photo Natura catalogue). Getty
Images: 8 (Kenneth Garrett/National Geographic),
10, 11 and 16 (Jane Burton/Dorling Kindersley
collection), 23 (Arthur Tilley/Taxi). Istockphoto:
title page and page 18, 4 (Justin Horrocks), 7, 12
(Mark Hayes), 13 (Alberto Perez Veiga), 20
(Beverley Vycital), 22 (Gregory Albertini).

Contents

What is a cat?

Cats that people keep as pets are known as **domestic cats**. They belong to a family of animals called **felids**. Some felids are much bigger than the domestic cat. These include lions and tigers.

▼ Cats are are very popular pets. They can make great companions.

Cats are meat-eating animals. Their bodies are well-suited to **hunting**. Cats can move quickly and quietly. They use their sharp claws and teeth to kill and eat their **prey**.

▲ Even a well-fed pet cat will hunt animals.

Wild cats

There are 36 different types of cat in the wild. Some are smaller than domestic cats. The European wildcat looks a lot like the domestic cat. It catches fish and hunts animals such as rabbits, mice and insects.

▼ This European wildcat is found in Scotland.

The largest members of the cat family include tigers, lions and leopards. Lions live together in groups, but most members of the cat family live alone.

▶ The Siberian tiger is the largest and heaviest type of tiger.

Cat Fact

The tiger is the biggest member of the cat family. Tigers can be more than 3 m long.

Domestic cats

People began keeping cats thousands of years ago. Cats would get rid of mice and rats in houses or farms. People also enjoyed having cats as companions.

Sometimes, domestic cats become homeless. They learn to survive without help from people. These cats and their **offspring** become half-wild. They are known as **feral cats**.

◀ This Egyptian statue is thousands of years old. The ancient Egyptians admired cats for their beauty and hunting skill.

▼ Feral cats live by hunting or on scraps they find. They often live together in groups to stay safe.

A kitten is born

Mother cats usually have between three and five **kittens** in a **litter**. Kittens are born with their eyes shut. They sleep huddled together to stay warm. They open their eyes when they are about ten days old.

▼ Newborn kittens feed on their mother's milk.

Kittens start walking at three weeks. At four weeks old, they begin to get teeth and can start eating solid food. At eight weeks old, a cat is ready to leave its mother.

▲ A mother cat uses her mouth to move her kittens.

Growing up

Kittens are very playful. They love to play with each other. They will also play with toys, paper bags and any pieces of string they find.

◀ Playing keeps a kitten fit. It is also good practice for hunting.

Cat Fact

The world's oldest cat lived for 38 years. Creme Puff lived in Texas, USA and died in 1997.

A cat is grown-up when it is between ten and twelve months old. Cats usually live for between nine and fifteen years. Some live into their twenties.

▼ Cats spend lots of time sleeping. They usually sleep for about sixteen hours a day.

Cat senses

Cats have a strong sense of smell. They also have very good hearing and eyesight. Cats see better than people at night. Whiskers can help a cat to get about at night too. The cat uses them to feel what is around it.

▲ Many pet cats like to go out hunting at night.

Cat Fact

A falling cat will twist its body so that it lands on its feet. It uses its great sense of balance to do this.

▲ Most cats love to climb. Their strong muscles and sharp claws make them good climbers.

Understanding cats

You can tell how a cat is feeling by watching it. A tail straight up means the cat is happy. An angry cat will flick his tail. A cat that is scared or ready to fight has a fluffed-up tail.

An angry cat may also hiss or growl. A happy cat usually makes a loud **purring** noise.

This cat is getting ready to scare off or attack an enemy.

▲ Cats meow at you to tell you they want something.

Many coats and colours

Cats can have many colours and markings. Special types of cat are called **breeds**. Most cats are a mixture of breeds.

▲ This Persian or Longhair cat has a flat face and long fur.

Some breeds have short, thick coats. Others have long fur. They may have different characters too. Some breeds are more friendly than others.

Cat Fact

The Sphynx is a strange breed of cat. It has hardly any fur and no whiskers.

◀ Siamese cats have dark faces, tails and paws. They usually have a very loud meow.

Choosing a pet cat

If you want a pet cat, you must be sure that you can care for it properly. Then you can decide what sort of cat to have. Do you want a kitten? Would you prefer to give a home to an older cat?

◀ Animal shelters have many cats that need good homes.

When you take your new cat to the vet, he or she will give it a health check.

A kitten will need to be **house trained**. This means teaching it to use a **litter tray**. Your pet will also need to see the vet for **vaccinations**. These will protect it from some diseases.

Caring for a cat

If you have a garden, a cat flap is a good idea. This allows your cat to come and go as it pleases. If your cat has to stay indoors, you must make sure it gets exercise.

Your pet cat will love to play games with you. Playing will stop it from getting bored and is a great way of spending time with your cat.

◄ Playing with toys is good exercise for cats of all ages.

A pet cat that is treated kindly will enjoy being with you.

Glossary

breed
A special type of cat. Cats of the same breed are very alike. This is because their parents were of the same type or breed.

domestic cat
Type of cat that lives with people and is kept as a pet.

felids
Family of animals that includes domestic cats, lions, tigers and wild cats.

feral cat
A cat that is half wild. Feral cats are usually domestic cats that have lost their homes or have been born to homeless cats.

house trained
A pet that has been trained to go to the toilet outside or in a special place, such as a litter tray.

hunt
To chase and kill an animal for food.

kitten
A young cat.

litter
The offspring, or young, born to an animal at one time.

litter tray
A tray that an animal uses as its toilet.

offspring
The young of an animal.

prey
An animal that is hunted by another animal for food.

purring
A vibrating sound that a cat makes in its throat. It usually does this when it is happy.

vaccination
An injection that is given to protect people or animals against some serious diseases.

Index